ON JIU JITSU

CHRIS MATAKAS

"Strength and Kindness." - *Noah Crome*

On Jiu Jitsu
Copyright © 2017 by Chris Matakas
Build The Fire Publishing
ISBN-13: 978-1546922902
ISBN-10: 1546922903

Edited by Kathy Matakas
Cover Photo by Eric Talerico
Cover Design by Mark Brehaut

BUILD THE FIRE
Publishing

For The Reader
May This Serve You Along Your Path

CONTENTS

PREFACE... 7

CHAPTER 1 - Why We Need Jiu Jitsu

    Statement of Purpose 11

    The Problem... 16

    The Solution... 18

CHAPTER 2- How We Grow

    Jiu Jitsu Trains Virtue, Removes Vice................. 28

    The Pairs of Virtue and Vice 35

    Humility and Pride... 38

    Resolve and Weakness... 54

    Efficacy and Ignorance 68

    Generosity.. 84

Chapter 3- Why We Grow

    Friendship 88

    Fellowship 93

    The Human Organism 96

CONCLUSION 104

PREFACE

I spent last summer alone in the national parks out west. I didn't train Jiu Jitsu once and rarely even thought about it. Deep down, I wasn't sure if I would ever train again.

I had been practicing Jiu Jitsu nearly every day, multiple times a day, for eight years. My body was broken, my soul was tired, and I wondered if teaching and training were still the best use of my single, finite life. With the blessing of my teacher, Professor Ricardo Almeida, I headed out on the greatest adventure of my life.

Having never camped before and rarely having driven beyond county limits, the 14,000-

mile trek and nearly every night spent sleeping under the stars in beautiful wilderness was a shock to the system; the experience my soul craved which my environment could not provide.

I went away to reassess. With nothing to attend to but my own mind, the freedom from my daily environment allowed me to determine my true values. I had no preconceived notions or hopes. I went away to get quiet and listen. Whatever I wanted to do at the end of the summer, that is how I would spend my life.

I soon realized that though I love nature, the smile of a friend is more beautiful than any mountain. People come first. After thirty years of cognitive dissonance, the path became clear. I chose the life I had been living, service to others through Jiu Jitsu.

Now I return to Jiu Jitsu with fresh eyes. My time away offered me a perspective that I so desperately needed. Jiu Jitsu, and its infinite complexity manifested through simplicity, would continue to be the tea ceremony through which I pursued perfection and the platform through which I strive to make a difference in the world.

I am certainly not qualified to speak about anything else, but luckily, nothing else is needed. The principles which constitute good grappling are the same which make for a good life: the acquisition of virtue and the removal of vice, as we gain a better understanding of our experience to maximize our effectiveness in the world.

Each of us stands to gain immeasurably from this study, as Jiu Jitsu has nothing to do with race, geography, or socio-economic standing and everything to do with developing the finer aspects of our nature.

Free of all social constraints, we come together in our shared ignorance and desire for a better understanding of ourselves and our world, and through the pragmatic study of subduing our fellow man, we learn to subdue the weaker aspects of our nature.

I believe that most activities we have ever enjoyed, whether a sport, an art, or a hobby, are so enjoyed because they deepen our relationship to ourselves. They free us of our daily concerns as we tunnel our attention toward one task, giving us a vehicle with which to strengthen our virtue while removing our weakness.

Jiu Jitsu is something different to each of us. Whatever our growth requires, it provides. We could practice every day for the rest of our lives and never exhaust its benefits. The capacity of limitations rests on our effort and awareness, not the craft.

Jiu Jitsu is a support system for life, daily shaping our character through the repetition of virtuous action, giving us the ability to act more nobly in the world. Its function within the human individual is to facilitate the development which brings us closer to our most actualized self.

I imagine that any activity, when practiced with sincerity, can achieve this aim. But we are not concerned with those activities; we are concerned with ours. Jiu Jitsu is not life, but it does open us to life in ways we often remain closed.

Jiu Jitsu is not the summit we aspire toward. It's the foundation we stand upon.

CHAPTER 1

Why We Need Jiu Jitsu

STATEMENT OF PURPOSE

The human individual derives much value from the practice of Brazilian Jiu Jitsu. I have never met a man or woman worse off for having trained. I never will. The transformative power of Jiu Jitsu is rare in that all aspects of the individual are trained: the body is taxed in every facet of athleticism, the mind is challenged to attend to countless variables as we navigate kinesthetic and proprioceptive challenges, and, perhaps most importantly, the soul is challenged to a degree which civilian life simply cannot offer within such a well-ordered and affluent society.

I have never found a single activity which so rivals its effectiveness to completely alter a person's life.

Philosophy sharpens the mind but does nothing for the body. Strength training builds the body but neglects the soul. But Jiu Jitsu attends to all of one's humanity. Jiu Jitsu helps many lose weight with success they never found at the gym. Jiu Jitsu improves our problem solving as no math tutor could. And Jiu Jitsu molds the character of a person with the same capacity as the highest place of worship.

The world is speeding up faster than any of us is ready for. Our attention is pulled in every direction. Our calendars are filled and our leisure is empty. We only have so much time for personal development, and with so much stimulus competing for our attention, we easily neglect fundamental aspects of our being.

But we are the lucky ones. We have found something we love which trains every aspect of our character, and often, without our intent to do so. Jiu Jitsu provides a medium with which to purposefully strengthen our weaknesses, willfully choosing discomfort and resistance over a passive life.

We channel the most primitive aspects of our nature toward the most sophisticated ends, practicing vulnerability and dominance with our fellow man, free of consequence.

Whether we are dominating or dominated, we learn the nature of cause and effect, receiving instant feedback with every experiment we make. This immediate feedback loop creates an accelerated growth that the common holding patterns of adult life cannot.

Jiu Jitsu allows us to pursue our highest selves which much of our waking lives suppress. We are so often pushed toward the middle and away from ourselves. Jiu Jitsu brings us back.

This book is not meant to improve your Jiu Jitsu. I have provided no philosophy regarding skill acquisition. Its sole purpose is to help you realize the wealth you already possess.

We tend to grow accustomed to the familiar to the point of blindness. Often, if we do not purposefully seek the value in something, we never find it. And sometimes the value is so ubiquitous that it goes unnoticed. My hopes are simply to remind you of the value that you have already found, to bring to conscious thought what you feel in your bones.

I have the tendency to think that who I am is who I always was, and in so doing, discredit the value and transformative nature of my experiences. Jiu Jitsu has been the victim of such myopic thinking. Jiu Jitsu has given me a quality of life I have never known. It has awoken me in ways I didn't know I was sleeping. I have never been so challenged-- physically, mentally, and emotionally-- through one medium. Jiu Jitsu has taught me a sincerity for purposefully directed study that academia did not.

I never had to choose Jiu Jitsu; it was thrust upon me. A friend urged me to take an introductory class, and an hour later, my path in life became clear. I never felt like I pursued Jiu Jitsu; it pursued me.

That has been the case with all the most meaningful aspects of my life. No push was necessary. I was pulled and had no say in the matter. Considering you, the reader, have taken time out of your day to read about Jiu Jitsu, I assume we share a similar experience.

Our continued practice of this art is so much more important than we often imagine. A purposeful reiteration of the task at hand ensures our success. When we become consciously aware of the value of our practice, we develop the antibodies with which to face adversity and overcome the vicissitudes which we will find along our path.

"He who has a great enough Why can withstand any How."
- Friedrich Nietzsche

When we consciously understand this truth, we free ourselves of the grind, and find a deep and passionate gratitude which propels our continued efforts. We happily make sacrifices to practice this art, because we realize they aren't sacrifices at all. Our finite time and energy, when put forth in Jiu Jitsu, has a greater return on investment than any area of human study.

We each stumbled upon this blessing. The articulation of its value is imperative. Increased understanding of the medium fosters an appreciation which provides the endurance to consistently strive toward our highest selves. The more clearly we understand this art, the more likely we are to use it wisely.

THE PROBLEM

Many today complain about the millennials. We criticize their work ethic, attention span, and their seeming aversion to effort as concern grows for the future of this country. But we forget the source of the modern dilemma.

The successes of those who come before paves the way for the weaknesses of those who follow. Generation after generation suffered as they ascended the hierarchy of human needs, and now with those needs met, we chastise the perceived weakness of a generation that had no battles from which to acquire strength.

> *"We will be soldiers, so our sons may be farmers, so their sons may be artists."*
> *- Thomas Jefferson*

We now understand that such noble striving comes at a cost. Without the need for exhaustive labor and sacrifice, our environment does not force us to develop the virtue our highest selves require.

We no longer hunt or grow food for our survival. Purified water is pumped into our homes which heat themselves. These are gifts from those who came before us, but these comforts come at an unseen cost.

The organism is shaped by the environment, and the environment is shaped by the organism. They go together, so much so that the philosopher Alan Watts combined the terms, "organism-environment." They are inextricably linked, the fate of one rests with the other.

In this modern world of convenience, in which our basic needs are met with minimal effort as we enjoy pleasurable distractions in abundance, we settle into the weakness which our environment allows.

> *"Somewhere along the line we seem to have confused comfort with happiness."*
> *- Dean Karnazes*

Since our environment doesn't demand our strength, we must ask it of ourselves. We do so to honor our latent potential. We are all capable of massive achievement and fulfillment, but with minimal external pressure to pursue such heights, we easily neglect these pursuits.

I have always viewed my life using the metaphor of a book. Is the life I live a story worth reading? My decisions strive to write a story I am proud to have lived. The highest self which authors such pages will be a product of massive, calculated effort toward a worthy ideal.

This highest self can only be found by pushing through repeated resistance. When our environment does not provide such opportunity, we are tasked to either change that environment or find a new one.

Happily, we need look no farther than Jiu Jitsu.

THE SOLUTION

Jiu Jitsu is unrivaled as a mechanism for personal development, as it best compliments individual and communal pursuits. Grappling challenges the mind, body, and soul of the practitioner with a functional capacity of the individual, not the medium.

But the real value is found in the mysticism of this practice.

Jiu Jitsu seems to offer far more than what it presents at face value. The ability to safely subdue an opponent seems to be the least valuable part of this practice. The average blue belt can safely defend himself against most assailants. One year of training leaves you at the upper echelon of humanity in martial combat.

Self-defense may be why many of us begin this practice but is rarely why we continue. Once we have met that criteria, which is met early, there must be a cause for the sacrifice we make in this continued practice. Our goals must transcend martial arts and enter the art of living.

Jiu Jitsu means something different to each of us and is malleable to one's individual needs. Two students can be practicing the same technique, in the same class under the same instruction, and be pursuing two starkly contrasting aspects of their experience. It is a vehicle which allows us to pursue a road uniquely our own, while traveling parallel with those whose path is anything but.

Like the many radii of the circle, we all begin in its center, and take this art to some distant periphery of which only we are capable. Jiu Jitsu's effectiveness is only limited by the degree we allow ourselves to be affected.

Two men can take the same classes, investing the equivalent hours, and one becomes a philosopher, the other a fighter. Some will recognize Jiu Jitsu as a tool for weight loss while the others will find the fellowship they have always sought but never found.

Jiu Jitsu becomes whatever we need it to be. The paradox is that we rarely acknowledge those needs until long after they have been met, as their presence illuminates their prior absence. I began training Jiu Jitsu because I wanted to be able to control an aggressor. I continue Jiu Jitsu because I seek to control myself.

Jiu Jitsu is something different to each of us but is the same for all of us. It is the mechanism with which we facilitate change and seek a better understanding of ourselves and our world.

We find a freedom of expression in which we manifest the virtues we lack. But again, we often don't know they are lacking until Jiu Jitsu provides the environment in which they grow, demanding a development of which we didn't know we were capable. It starts with our soul and works outward. We think we are learning to fight, but we are learning to live.

Jiu Jitsu allows us to dive deeper into ourselves in a world that is striving to keep us on the surface. Its complexity reveals our own. Its mastery is a mastery of self.

Jiu Jitsu provides an understanding of causality so rare to our experience. We are given instant feedback in a constant dance between action and reaction. I go for an arm drag from butterfly guard and my partner only has a few common responses. I act accordingly based off their reaction and achieve my intended aim. There is beauty in this linear and discernible transactional nature.

The causality which guides all experience, but so often remains hidden, becomes visible.

We tend to define the external world as something foreign to ourselves, and readily ascribe much of circumstance to chance. But underneath this seemingly endless multiplicity lies a unity of causation. There is a thread which weaves throughout all of experience and Jiu Jitsu reveals this.

In the same way that my attacks from butterfly guard follow a linear trajectory comprised of finite variables, life follows the same path. Everything is a result of everything else, and when we tunnel our vision to a specific area of our lives, the sea of seemingly infinite possibility becomes identifiable.

Jiu Jitsu no longer allows me to claim woeful ignorance. I can no longer blame fate for my circumstance or chance for my hardships. Each phenomenon is preceded and followed by a link in the chain; we just need to develop the lens to see that chain to which we are bound.

We are not poor because of our employer; we are poor because of our decisions. We are not overweight because of our metabolism; we are unhealthy because we practice unhealthy habits. Our blessings and shortcomings do not exist on an island. Jiu Jitsu reveals there are no islands.

Everything is governed by causality. Jiu Jitsu has shown us that everything can be understood. We simply need to understand the mechanisms of understanding.

Jiu Jitsu affords us the opportunity to suffer with purpose. This suffering creates a mental strength which, like any skill, must be practiced. The countless benefits of the civilized world have made our lives comfortable, but the very nature of comfortability requires no strength.

The strong man, if not asked to use his strength, will become weak. We must not fall into the trap of thinking we are strong because we once were.

Jiu Jitsu gives us daily opportunities to confront difficulty. When training with skilled opponents, we find ourselves in experiences which test our character. When a guard pass is resisted, when we are caught in a deep arm bar or in a great scramble, we are presented with a choice: yield or press on.

This is one of the greatest gifts of Jiu Jitsu. The gift our souls most need.

Adult life is being at the mercy of our own habits in a culture whose stream is flowing toward the middle: a common ground requiring minimal growth and strength, often deterring such progress.

Stand up. Sit down. Be quiet. Buy this.

When training Jiu Jitsu, we purposefully put ourselves in positions to grow. Jiu Jitsu strengthens our resolve because it demands resolution. One simply cannot practice Jiu Jitsu optimally while harboring weakness. Jiu Jitsu is too perfect to be bastardized by our imperfections.

> *"There is only one thing that I dread: not to be worthy of my sufferings."*
> *- Fyodor Dostoevsky*

The great men of history were only as strong as the depths of their suffering. Jiu Jitsu allows us to suffer with a purpose, ensuring we cultivate the strength to live for one.

This living for a purpose is a daily struggle to exceed one's self. We strive to go to bed at night slightly better than when we woke that morning, to know that we used our time well toward a worthy cause. But to do so means we must have a sound understanding of that cause and the lifetime of choices which will foster its creation.

We must do our best today, but that best is defined by our vision of a distant tomorrow. Often, the choices which best serve that future are the ones we least enjoy making today.

Our culture does not value health. We lead sedentary, fast food-filled, screen-based lives. Our daily experience requires minimal attention toward one's health. Jiu Jitsu, however, requires all of it.

Jiu Jitsu forces me to take time out of every day to do my corrective work. Pulling sleds, lying on softballs, and hanging upside down each morning are a small penance to pay for a pain-free life. But I don't do this as a responsible adult concerned with aging. I suffer today so I can train tomorrow. Jiu Jitsu provides an urgency which visions of my 80-year-old self never could.

And, it turns out, the immediate reward of getting to train Jiu Jitsu seems to be the governing force behind most of my right decisions. I eat a healthy breakfast, not to look good this summer, but to feel good in training. I get to bed early not to diminish the bags under my eyes, but to recover from practice. I stretch not to be flexible, but to be flexible for Jiu Jitsu.

Professor Almeida often advocates competing because the sense of urgency forces us to be sharper and more disciplined. What competing does for our Jiu Jitsu, Jiu Jitsu does for our lives. Jiu Jitsu gives us a persuasive reason to adopt the most optimal behavior.

I can think of no more worthwhile metric for our passions than this:

> *That which inspires one to pursue his highest self, losing himself and human weakness along the way, through complete immersion in a medium; when one cannot be distracted by the world because he has created his own; a more vivid, real existence in the expression of himself through his chosen pursuit.*

The value of a passion or hobby is found in the meaning it gives one's life and the growth it fosters in the individual. This is what Jiu Jitsu has done for many of us, giving us a greater sincerity than we have known, as we willingly trade our finite existence to explore its depths.

This conscious choice to dedicate one's self toward a worthy end is paramount.

> *"Here is something else that's weird but true. In the day to day trenches of adult existence, there is no such thing as atheism. Everyone worships, the only question is what to worship."*
> *-David Foster Wallace*

"Worship" holds strong connotations, but I believe it is an accurate term to articulate the reverence and adoration with which we lose ourselves in this art. We are fortunate to have made this choice ourselves, before advertising and common culture did it for us.

Ultimately, we each commit our lives to something. With Jiu Jitsu, we know our efforts are rewarded. We devote our attention and energy toward this medium and are given more in return than we ever put forth.

This reward comes in the form of who we become. There is no greater investment than one's own being. To better understand Jiu

Jitsu's value, we must understand the specific aspects of our being which are so fundamentally transformed. The more directly we can articulate this truth, the more likely we are to acknowledge this transformation when it occurs and continue our practice.

In the daily struggle for our lives, we need every advantage possible. Having consciously chosen terms with which to measure experience can make all the difference. When we label the finer aspects of our being, we provide ourselves with a means of viewing experience through the lens of something greater. We come to see our experience for what it really is, what it always was-- basic training for the soul.

CHAPTER 2

How We Grow

JIU JITSU TRAINS VIRTUE, REMOVES VICE

I have always been more concerned with who I was becoming rather than what I was achieving. Therefore, I fell in love with Jiu Jitsu-- a perfect medium to seek continued self-development, as every partner and position offers growth-inducing resistance.

There is much value to be found in the teachings of the Stoics. Stoicism is an ancient philosophy which teaches self-mastery to become impervious to the hands of fate. The Stoics viewed daily life as a training ground in which we constantly strive to acquire virtue and remove vice.

Much of the modern world has gotten away from this focus, as we seem to invest more in acts themselves than who we become through their performance. Virtue so rarely becomes a topic of conversation, and if we are not discussing virtue, odds are we are not pursuing it, either.

The great teachers of virtue left behind many books on the theory of its cultivation. The practice, however, falls upon us. Our actions in the world are the avenues by which we practice that Stoic philosophy, purposefully seeking virtue in route to our highest selves.

Real world experience molds the soul more than any book. Jiu Jitsu, out of sheer necessity, forces the practitioner to daily sharpen his virtue and remove his vice. If we do not adapt, we cannot advance in this art. Jiu Jitsu provides the practical benefits of ancient philosophy, free from labor-intensive academia.

We come to embody the most noble philosophies without ever attempting to do so. This reveals the most fundamental benefit of our Jiu Jitsu training:

The Jiu Jitsu academy is the one place in our lives where we purposefully practice virtue.

I am always in awe of the quality of people who gather on our mats each morning. Men who have achieved the greatest heights in the most dangerous and competitive fields. UFC Champions. IBJJF World Champions. ADCC Veterans.

But the pedigree of students in the night classes is just as impressive. Amazing moms. Dedicated fathers. High achievers in business. Young men and women who abstain from culture's influence and pursue something better, demonstrating a wisdom foreign to most of us at that age. And I am not surprised. The traits needed to succeed in Jiu Jitsu are the same that our highest humanity requires.

There seems to be a natural progression of personal development. First, you do the work on yourself so you become more. Then, you give away what you have become in the service of others. Until, finally, your continued service removes the separations between man which creates the "other," and you see yourselves as part of a larger, unified whole.

That's the progression:
Me. We. Everyone.

And the achievement of this progression, whether in Jiu Jitsu or in our humanity, is grounded in the development of four virtues and the removal, to whatever extent we are capable, of three vices.

The virtues: Humility, Resolve, Efficacy, and Generosity.
The vices: Pride, Weakness, and Ignorance.

These are the fundamental aspects of our character which Jiu Jitsu trains. These terms, virtue and vice, allow us to quantify aspects of the human experience which are by nature ambiguous. By naming them, we are able to repeatedly recognize these motivating forces from our depths which manifest on the surface through our actions. These terms are the measuring stick of character development.

If you don't like these specific terms, grab a thesaurus and choose any word of similar meaning you'd prefer. The words don't matter. Your soul does.

The labels allow us an awareness to bring these aspects of our character to the forefront of our minds, where we shape them to our will, through conscious repetition guided by massive effort and awareness.

We have no excuses for our shortcomings because we have never truly tried to change them. We pay them lip service, sure. Maybe we even apply some haphazard effort to effect change. But our effort is applied inefficiently, inconsistently, and without full intention.

This apathy is contrasted with our action in Jiu Jitsu. Consider when you are working on a specific technique in training. You watch YouTube videos before rolling, you devote that entire training session to getting reps practicing that technique against a resisting partner, and then, after training, you seek the counsel of everyone on the mat who might have valuable input regarding that technique, followed by copious notetaking.

When was the last time we were so intent on the cultivation of our character? Imagine the type of people we would become if we were as purposeful about the removal of vice.

Before leaving the house for work, we read ancient scripture and philosophy about quelling the ego. We study this first thing, so when we enter the world, we are primed to behave in the most conducive way to achieve our aim of removing pride. We treat every person we interact with as an opportunity to "get reps" in a live setting. Then, throughout the day, we seek the counsel of those around us who embody that trait we wish to develop and maybe even take some notes on the day's progress before retiring for the night.

But this doesn't seem excessive. Jiu Jitsu has shown us that this is the most efficient and effective way to improve our grappling.

We should be even more purposeful when developing our humanity.

First, I envision an academy in which all students have a notebook: tracking what they are working on, the experiences they are having, and the nuggets worth holding onto. This is a community of sincere practitioners.

And once we can do this in our Jiu Jitsu academies, we could live this way in the world. We would then carry around notebooks tracking our progress toward virtue and away from vice; noting when we have fallen short of our ideal, acknowledging when others embody those virtues we seek to develop.

> *"What gets measured, gets managed."*
> *- Peter Drucker*

The most important aspects of life, those grounded in the love of others and our passions, rarely have quantifiable metrics. Becoming more kind is difficult to quantify. You receive no trophy for growing in appreciation of your friend's accomplishments.

Interestingly, we have no measurements for that which is most worth measuring. It is our virtues which we seek to train and vices we seek to remove. These are the gatekeepers to our highest selves.

Our weakness shackles the Providence within us. Our virtue allows it to shine forth. We have much more say in the matter than we acknowledge. We have the ability to craft the fabric of our being. We are not limited by circumstance. We are limited by ourselves.

Devoting our attention to our depths radically alters the surface. We must purposefully seek character development just as we pursue improved guard passing. Jiu Jitsu forces us to train our character in the precise way our humanity requires. With complete transference, the virtues we embody on the mat take root in our daily lives.

THE PAIRS OF VIRTUE AND VICE

Life is full of seeming contradictions. Cognitive dissonance, dichotomies and polarities litter the streets of our common language. We say, "Absence makes the heart grow fonder," but with our next breath proclaim, accurately, that "Time heals all wounds."

There is a truth in opposites. They go together. And though they seem separate, they are connected in ways we can't easily understand.

> *"Really, the fundamental, ultimate mystery-- the only thing you need to know to understand the deepest metaphysical secrets-- is this: that for every outside there is an inside and for every inside there is an outside, and although they are different, they go together."*
> *- Alan Watts*

When I set out to write this book, I wrote every day about Jiu Jitsu. I didn't know what kind of book I was writing. I just showed up to the blank page and wrote whatever came to mind. When I ran out of words, I put all the separate files into a single document and read the meandering ramblings in search of a connecting thread.

Only very late in the creative process did I realized what this book was. The writing centered around a common theme: using Jiu Jitsu as a tool for personal development. But this is vague and esoteric. Looking closer, I observed that most of the advantages of grappling seemed to be grounded in three pairs of opposites.

Humility and Pride.
Resolve and Weakness.
Efficacy and Ignorance.

Nearly everything I had written danced around these themes, with my complete lack of intention to do so. These core pairings constitute the bulk of character development. The acquisition of these virtues, and the removal of these vices, seems to be the bridge between the life we live and the live we dream of.

The sages and saints of the past have always embodied these virtues and made great advancements in the removal of these vices. They operated from a place of humility, recognizing there are powers at work, deep within themselves, far greater than who they so commonly perceive themselves to be. As Aldous Huxley taught, "For God's kingdom to come, our kingdom must go."

With this openness, they all possess a resolve with which they face adversity and suffering, transforming obstacles into the foundation of their character development.

Having done so, they are now capable of shaping their world through efficacy. These are the three virtues Jiu Jitsu most trains. Your ego is removed. Your soul is strengthened. And you become capable of manifesting change in the world.

By a fortuitous turn of events, Grace has given us a tool which trains the virtues our being most requires. This is the foundation for a good life. Without even meaning to do so, we have come to an art whose mastery demands the master of our humanity.

What a gift.

If we are to achieve our potential, if we are to have something to give others, we must learn to get out of our own way through an understanding of our first pair, Humility and Pride.

HUMILITY AND PRIDE

A truly humble man has no concept of his humility, for he cannot fathom that he would be so special to have the need to be humble. He is too busy getting lost in appreciation of a craft or his fellow man to think of himself.

> *"True humility is not thinking less of yourself; it is thinking of yourself less."*
> *- C.S. Lewis*

The prideful man thinks only of himself. Those external to him are nothing more than a measuring stick with which he raises his self-worth. Acting from this center, we shape our world and the lives of those around us with this fundamental choice, directing our gaze, either inward or outward.

Where you fall on the continuum of humility and pride is an infallible metric of the quality of your experience. It is our responsibility, to ourselves and to each other, to daily strive toward the more noble end of this continuum.

The *Perennial Philosophy*, popularized by Huxley in his book of the same title, the principle found at the foundation of all spiritual and religious teachings, is a removal of self through union with something greater than one's self.

Our own experience reveals this truth. If you want to feel good, focus on other people. Our suffering increases in proportion to the extent we focus on ourselves.

We are all familiar with the religious connotations of pride as a deadly sin. The best definition of sin, at least for my own comprehension, is that which removes us from God. If you prefer a different vocabulary, replace the word God with whatever name you use to describe the indescribable-- the Divine Ground, the Atman, the Tao, the universe-- that which is far greater than ourselves and of which we are a small part.

Verbiage aside, the less we focus on ourselves, the more we come to know that mystery. Thankfully, Jiu Jitsu forces us to seek value beyond ourselves, loosening the grip of our inward focused tendencies.

If one is to improve his Jiu Jitsu, he must operate from a place of openness and receptivity, constantly seeking the counsel of others to come to a better understanding of the craft. The complexity of our craft forces us to borrow the lens of others, relying on their viewpoint to construct our own.

Pride is the greatest impediment to our improvement. No one will teach you that which you claim to know, and if we cling tightly, we fail to learn from our greatest teacher of all, experience.

Jiu Jitsu demands that we humble ourselves. Whether we are guided or dragged, we are forced to confront this aspect of our psyche, acknowledging our shortcomings and learning to let go of ourselves on the way to something greater.

HUMILITY

Other than Professor Almeida, I am usually the most tenured person on the mat, and yet, I am surrounded by teammates who all understand certain aspects of grappling better than I do.

With finite mat time and subjective propensities, we each explore a limited portion of Jiu Jitsu. In a room of dedicated students, everyone understands an aspect of grappling better than we do.

Many of my immediate teachers are technically my junior, and this is the lesson:

> *You can be senior in rank, relative to your teammate, while being junior in your understanding of a position, technique, or concept.*

I think far too often as students ascend the belt ranks, they create a mental blockade in which, once someone is a lower rank than them, they assume they can no longer learn from that person. Though rarely a conscious choice, there seems to be a natural resistance to openly listening to someone who is designated your junior.

Everyone knows something you don't. Our rolls tend to follow similar trajectories. The more time we spend mastering one type of game, the less time we leave for the practice of alternative styles. As each of us comes to Jiu Jitsu with our unique lens, with a coupling of genetic predispositions and life experiences, we gain a perspective which exists solely within us.

The aim of Jiu Jitsu is to subdue another using your body. This is the goal we all share and yet we pursue its end in such contrasting ways.

Plato had this idea that everything was a manifestation of a perfect Form, an ideal version of that thing, existing beyond space and time. He believed that each chair was a reflection of that ideal chair, with all manifestations falling short of that perfection.

This way of thinking serves many purposes; Jiu Jitsu is not one of them. There is no universal form of Jiu Jitsu. The quality of its expression depends upon the practitioner, who acts within his own strengths and weaknesses, leaving him, if he is of great skill, optimally equipped to perform a particular style of game, relying on a sub-section of techniques within various positions, best performed by a body of his specific attributes.

By achieving perfection in one style of play, we lose it in all others. The opportunity cost of greatness is to be truly great in something but nothing else.

There is no universal form of Jiu Jitsu, because no human vehicle can be best suited to excel in every style of game play, as it is our differences which create the so many contrasting styles of play. We are each confined, to paraphrase Thoreau, by the narrowness of our experience.

These various proclivities and inclinations result in each of our attentions being pulled in different directions, finding success with techniques, concepts, and positions in which we are best fashioned to do so. We each go farther and farther down our own rabbit hole, creating games which are appropriate representations of the contrasting depths we all possess below the surface.

In a room full of experienced grapplers, everyone knows something you do not. You may have a training partner you whoop every day, but that doesn't mean your understanding has surpassed his in every aspect of grappling. He is simply unable to perform where he is better than you, on you, because you so surpass him everywhere else. We impede our own education.

Here my friend possesses a wonderful treasure, and because of my shortsightedness, I never see it. If we are to glimpse our potential, we must learn to see everyone as teachers.

The most experienced grappler in the room is probably the one asking the most questions.

Each of us represents a very minimal understanding of Jiu Jitsu. This is a blessing. It's not hard to radically improve every day. Jiu Jitsu is as vast as we are limited. The experienced student has just enough knowledge to illuminate his ignorance.

If I am unable to teach a seminar about one specific position or concept, without any prep time, then I do not fully understand that area of grappling. There is a big difference between knowing something in your head and feeling it in your bones. When I consider how I understand guard passing, and I recognize that the same amount of knowledge (and so much more) can be had in every position, technique, or concept, I am aware that I have barely glimpsed the depths of Jiu Jitsu.

The farther we go down the road, the more we realize just how much farther there is to travel. Our knowledge reveals our ignorance.

> *"I do not know what I may appear to the world, but to myself I seem to have been only like a boy playing on the seashore, and diverting myself in now and then*

finding a smoother pebble or a prettier shell than ordinary, whilst the great ocean of truth lay all undiscovered before me."
- Isaac Newton

And this is the transformative power of Jiu Jitsu. Our awareness of ignorance on the mat allows us to more easily recognize this truth in our daily lives. Admitting the shortcomings of our lens leaves us more inclined to benefit from the perspective of others.

This is best expressed using the Zen Koan:

One day, the great Zen master received a visit from his most renowned student. Though brilliant and worldly successful, this student was bound up by ego and full of pride.

The master served tea. He filled his student's cup to the brim, and then kept on pouring.

The student watched as the cup overflowed, making a mess all over the kitchen table. Finally, he could no longer restrain himself as he yelled, "The cup is full. No more will go in!"

Calmly, the master set down the teapot.

"Like this cup," he said, "You are full of your own beliefs and opinions. How can I show you Zen unless you first empty your cup?"

We are most willing to empty our cups while on the mats. Our love of grappling becomes the impetus for our improved humanity. We acquire daily reps of self-emptying in seeking the council of others. We do it first on the mat and then in the world. When we embody this openness, we remove our greatest impediment to education, ourselves. It is only then that we can truly receive others' teachings.

So much of education is learning to unlearn what we acquire along the way. But we are hesitant to empty our cups because we define ourselves by what's inside.

Jiu Jitsu has a built-in mechanism for humility: our inherent lack of skill in combat.

We've all seen the YouTube videos of street fights. Even amateur mixed martial arts, with men and women devoting their lives to combat, can make one cringe. And, after one's first round of live training with an experienced student, our lack of skill becomes clear. We have no problems emptying our cup when a man half our size does it for us.

And this is the gift. When we are constantly humbled on the mat, daily letting go of our notions of superiority, we can acknowledge when we stumble in the rest of our lives. Character development transcends disciplines. We bring the humility we find in grappling into the rest of our lives.

We require courage to empty our cup. And it requires courage to simply sit down for tea. Everyone on the mat has chosen a life of difficulty through this art. While so many spend the night in front of the television, we spend ours striving toward our highest selves.

It takes tremendous courage to step on the mat for the first time. You earn a white belt by having the bravery to embark on this worthy endeavor. Humility is required to recognize that you want something out of life which you do not currently possess: a better body, the ability to defend one's self, fellowship, or simply a hobby.

This heroic and honest assessment of one's self is only made possible through humility. The prideful man would never embark on such an endeavor which requires the help of so many. We come to a Jiu Jitsu academy because we realize we cannot go at it alone, that our development requires the assistance of a community.

Whatever it is we search for, we find it, and bring it with us into the rest of our lives. In every hero's journey, the protagonist descends to that special world, wins the boon, and brings it back to share in the ordinary world with his contemporaries. We are no different, but rather than return with some magic sword or potion, we return with strength and kindness.

A strength and kindness which can only be found when one admits his struggle and shortcomings, and in yielding to the teachings of wiser men, loses one's self in a worthy endeavor to become something more.

Humility frees us of our self-imposed limitations by helping us repeatedly find value outside of ourselves, and coming to an awareness that if we are to achieve anything, our success is due to all those who cross our path.

PRIDE

Pride is the opposite of humility. Where humility opens one's self, pride bolts the door shut. Pride is too busy raising one's self-perception to acknowledge that others have something to offer.

Pride causes us to see others not as they are, but as they are relative to us. Pride is the measuring stick: the way we determine our relative value to our fellow man. This value comes at a great cost; we raise our self-worth by lowering our esteem of others. We think too little of our neighbor and too much of ourselves.

Pride is the defense of an illusion which impedes all that is real. Our inner monologue strives to constantly build our self-esteem, a castle of self-worth built on the sands of subjective, inaccurate judgments of others.

Pride is a fixed mindset, a rigid definition and defending of what one is. Pride is closed off. But humility is open and allows a looseness of form. A growth mindset is possible because one takes an honest and detached assessment of what one is, therefore allowing one to become more.

Jiu Jitsu does not allow for pride. Everyone begins as a white belt. Our inadequacy leaves nothing for pride to cling to. When we are green and possess no understanding of the art, it is indistinguishable from magic, as our partner moves the two of us in a dance that we don't understand, taking us to a point of finality without realizing how we got there.

We simply become too confused to still think highly of ourselves. A world of profound depth reveals itself. We are intrigued. We have just had a sorcery performed on us that requires no magic, just continued effort and attention. Then we realize, we possess the ability to replicate any technique which is done to us.

As our partner manipulates us at his discretion, he is teaching us our own possibilities. But in revealing the possible, they reveal what we are not. Our ignorance is too omnipresent to warrant any semblance of false pride.

We are brought to the sudden realization that we know very little.

It is said that during his time, Socrates was proclaimed the world's wisest man by the Oracle of Delphi. Upon hearing this, Socrates was skeptical, for he knew the extent of his finite understanding. He went from great thinker to great thinker, interviewing all of them in search of a man wiser than he. He eventually came to the realization that the oracle was right.

He was the wisest man, not because of what he knew, but because he seemed to be the only one who could admit what he did not know.

Jiu Jitsu thrusts our ignorance upon us daily. Its infinite complexity can never be grasped by our finite minds. We are too limited. It is too vast. The longer one trains the more clear this truth becomes. We can never come to know its heights. At best, for mere moments, we perform an aspect of Jiu Jitsu perfectly, free of all our weakness. We have not conquered Jiu Jitsu. We merely stood worthy of the art for a brief moment.

Again, we cannot underestimate what this does to a human psyche. When one's limitations are so clearly placed before him, he begins to question himself in other areas as well. He comes to know that his relationships, profession, and other interests possess just as much unseen depth.

Virtues and vices are not limited to specific arenas. If one has pride in his soul, it will seek to manifest itself in his every endeavor. In the context of character development, how we do one thing is how we do all things, because the aspect of our being we exercise toward one end, we bring with us into all others.

If you humble yourself enough times, pride dies. For some of us it only takes a few follies and we get the message. Others will fail endlessly and somehow cling to their prideful ways to which we are so averse. But in time, if they have enough experiences, they will learn.

The steepness of the Jiu Jitsu learning curve is just too high. If we are to ascend, we can bring nothing with us. If we are to master Jiu Jitsu and ourselves, we must learn to diminish, and maybe someday remove, our pride.

Pride, the constant defense of one's self image, impedes our ability to see the beauty within ourselves. Our ego tries to paint the picture others see, doing so with a fraction of the capabilities of our full organism, that which is painting the canvas of our lives in every moment. Whatever we tell ourselves we are, deep down, we are so much more. But we will never come to know those depths if we keep shouting how great we are while on the surface.

SUMMARY OF HUMILITY AND PRIDE

Our first coupling is simply a matter of openness. Are we receptive to the blessings which our environment offers? Each of us has such a limited capacity for understanding, growth, and effectiveness in the world. We all represent a tiny sliver of the lens of humanity. We see a small piece of the whole, never grasping its entirety.

Pride is a self-worth derived from devaluing others. We denigrate our fellow man, the source of our greatest connection and education. Our limitations demand that we seek the assistance of others to achieve our continued growth.

Humility is the doorway through which all education enters. Pride shuts that door, bolts it tight, and like a small child covering his ears and shouting over his parent's words, impedes our ability to learn from the wisdom of others.

Pride shackles us to a lower existence. Humility sets us free.

RESOLVE AND WEAKNESS

Where we reside on the humility-pride continuum determines our ability to interact with the world. We cannot have a relationship with experience if we are too busy constructing a false relationship to ourselves.

This is the battle of self. But this self is forged and strengthened through resolve in the face of daily adversity. Our ability to continually meet resistance in the most productive way determines how close we come to our potential.

Whether you are a steward of your abilities, or actively stifling your potential, depends upon where you lie on the resolve-weakness continuum.

Our highest selves are found on the far side of a lifetime of choosing continuous effort in the face of resistance. How we meet that resistance, today and twenty years from now, shapes who we become. Knowing that every action is an expression of our deepest nature, do we press on in the face of difficulty, or do we yield?

This decision depends upon a man's resolve-- the endurance to consistently make the right choice amid fatigue and discomfort.

The quality of choice we make in this moment is a product of the quantity of choices we have made prior. Our resolve muscles need reps to grow.

Jiu Jitsu crams a month worth of these repetitions into a single training session. There is no ceiling for the training of virtues; a saint who lives a hundred years will never become the savior he aspires to be. It's just too far out of reach. He can still improve those aspects of his character which already surpass most men. There are no limitations in carving our soul. Our depths cannot be fully known.

Whoever gets the most reps, and makes the most of these opportunities through choosing effort over passivity, achieves the height of these virtues. Our cultivation of these gifts is contingent upon the amount of reps we can acquire, and our ability to make the most of these opportunities by choosing effort over passivity, seeking constructive pain over deconstructive pleasures.

The more times we confront this inevitable choice, yield or press on, the stronger our powers of decision-making become. A Jiu Jitsu academy becomes the environment which forces the adaptation of our character by giving us these reps, acting as the proving ground of the soul on which modern life has paved a parking lot.

> *Vice in abundance is easy to get,*
> *The road is smooth and begins beside you, But the gods have put sweat between us and virtue, And a road that is long, rough, and steep.*
> *- Hesiod*

RESOLVE

The practice of Jiu Jitsu is the cultivation of resolve. Jiu Jitsu presents limitless problem sets and each one has an optimal solution. Our training partners offer resistance against our will. Every moment we meet adversity as we strive to achieve our intended result. Constantly facing this difficulty in the most productive way ensures the development of a character capable of facing any worldly circumstance.

We each come prepackaged with certain propensities and abilities. There are certain activities we are meant to do and others we are not. At 5'8" and mediocre athleticism, I was never meant to play professional sports which require the size, speed, and strength of premier athletes.

But Jiu Jitsu is different. There is no set way to practice Jiu Jitsu. We are afforded limitless variables and styles of gameplay with which to fashion a game which best suits our abilities and disposition. If we have the requisite level of athleticism and intelligence to practice this art, then our success in its proper application is possible.

There exists a game in which you can excel. And if there doesn't, you are free to invent one. Jiu Jitsu's perfection is not limited by our imperfection.

This means that we can each achieve a high level of mastery unique to our experience within the confines of our subjective strengths and weaknesses.

If we are born slow, then we can cultivate a game that does not require speed. The same holds true with every other physical characteristic. We are finally free to play free of our weakness. This leaves no room for self-doubt or blaming circumstance, as the lot we inherit is exactly what is needed for our optimal performance.

Mastery is accessible in Jiu Jitsu in a way it is not in the rest of our lives. Our physical limitations become our strengths, the foundation of our particular game for which we are best suited. For many, we have found the first arena in which we can be truly masterful.

If we work hard, intelligently, and over extended duration, we can achieve the mastery of which only we are capable. Success is guaranteed because success is possible. We are free to come as close to our perfection as we wish.

This true potential for success creates a resolve that only comes from certainty, a confidence in walking a path for which only you are fashioned. When we realize this certainty of success in grappling, we come to understand its prevalence in the rest of our lives.

We each possess a rare combination of strengths and weaknesses, but for most of us, a general competency of most skills is possible. Adequacy is achievable through mindful repetition.

A certain amount of reps separates us from our ability to perform a task well. Sometimes we are fashioned to do that task, and we only need a handful of experiences to have a firm grasp of the skill.

Other times, competency eludes us, and we require hundreds of reps to achieve a basic level of skill. No matter where we lie on this continuum, a functional level of success is possible, assuming we meet our requisite reps.

In the same way our mastery is ensured in grappling through continued effort, the same holds true for the rest of our humanity. Our success may come soon, or in years, but it will come if we stay the course, applying consistent, intelligent effort.

The resolve which we show in Jiu Jitsu, leading to our unique form of mastery, is the same resolve which allows us to achieve skill in any other area of our lives.

Our opportunity for success in grappling reveals an opportunity for success in all the activities. *I'm not good at that.* Nonsense. You have a high number of repetitions necessary to achieve mastery, and you have yet to achieve that number. Meet that number and you'll find your skill.

We aren't "bad" at anything. We just haven't practiced enough. Skill development requires a resolve which frees us of that detrimental internal dialogue and allows us to collect the necessary reps to achieve the skill of which we are capable.

The resolve that we have learned from pushing through adversity on the mats translates everywhere else. The day's load lightens as we strengthen our discipline muscles.

WEAKNESS

The opposite of this resolve is weakness. Weakness is a broad term, but succinct in the expression of all those times we choose the easy path over the right path, when we choose complacency over advancement, when we yield rather than press on.

We are weak when we are unkind to others. We are weak when we are unkind to ourselves. We are weak when we respond to the uncontrollable events in our lives with resentment and bitterness. We are weak during those subtle choices throughout the day which gradually impeded the achievement of our highest selves.

Our modern environment does not punish such weakness, thus highlighting our need for Jiu Jitsu-- the environment in which success demands a sharpening of resolve and the daily stripping away of our self-imposed limitations.

Jiu Jitsu gives the practitioner a medium with which to confront his weaknesses. Every moment of a role is an opportunity to face adversity, push through mental limitations, and put forth massive effort toward a predetermined goal, all against an ever-changing resistance which wants just as badly for you to fail as you wish to succeed.

Training offers instant feedback for our vices in a way that our daily lives never can. That extra cup of coffee each day, television before bed, avoiding difficult conversations with your partner, often do not show their effects until it is too late. But we aren't able to have the same negligence in Jiu Jitsu; immediate data reveals our folly.

If we are sloppy and lead with our neck while passing, we get choked. If we are lazy in hand-fighting, our guard gets passed. Let your partner keep that grip on your wrist too long, and you get swept. We are immediately punished for our weaknesses, and if we are attentive to the laws of causality, we can quickly recognize what causes us to fail and what steps must be taken next time to ensure success.

Your training partner serves as your accountability partner. It is this interdependence within the community which accelerates our growth. While training with our peers, every time we act sub-optimally, our partner capitalizes on our misstep and exposes our mistake. Our weaknesses are constantly exposed.

Adult life offers none of this. No one puts veggies on your plate. There is no television curfew. No one is pulling the phone out of our hand. The guidance we've outgrown has been usurped by the freedom in which our bad habits take root.

These habits easily go unnoticed, as everyone else is as sincerely focused on their own lives as we are ours. No one is really watching us that closely. And with each of us walking a unique path, there is really no way to know what each other needs in our own unique development. Who am I to say my friend shouldn't play video games? Maybe that provides the rest his development most requires.

Without an agreed upon metric, the path toward success can often become unclear. But Jiu Jitsu has an agreed upon set of goals. Concrete metrics within a limited field of variables easily distinguish between success and failure.

Sweep. Pass. Submit. This is our aim.

When these values are shared between two training partners, they are each working toward the exact same goal and thus there is no room for ambiguity in the results. Sweep your partner, pass his guard and submit him and you have bested him in that round; you have achieved the aim you each pursued but only you achieved. You won. He lost.

Jiu Jitsu offers a very simple set of rules to which we all adhere, thus allowing our partner to add maximum resistance in exact opposition to our desires. The lack of subjective interpretation creates an environment which maximizes our growth through easily accessible resistance.

But in daily life we possess no commonly agreed upon metric for success. Our values are uniquely our own. Our desired ends are as different as we are. If you have a long day, who's to say that watching television to unwind isn't a good use of your time?

We can rationalize this action without external friction. We do this all day. Maybe I choose to heat up pasta rather than make a salad. *I could use the carbs for training tomorrow.* Maybe I don't do my corrective work that day. *One day off won't hurt.*

And this is the problem. We have very few safeguards to protect us from our own human weakness. Weakness which manifests itself in the subtle choices we make hundreds of times a day; those mundane, minute decisions which shape our world as they insidiously nudge us off our path.

But Jiu Jitsu leaves no room for weakness. If we get tired and move in a lazy fashion mid-roll, we get submitted. If we do not pay close attention to our partner's grips, we get our guard passed. If we go for a risky move at an improper time, our partner capitalizes.

By the simple nature of the feedback loop, we are rewarded for our proper actions and punished for our inefficiencies. If we make the same mistake while guard passing a few times in a row, our weakness becomes glaringly obvious. But a similar mistake in real life can go unnoticed for a lifetime. *That always happens to me*, we say, never realizing we repeatedly fail to learn the same lesson.

There is great value in purposefully meeting resistance each day. This is why so many of us enjoyed athletics growing up. We used our sports as vehicles to mold our character, as each offers resistance and fatigue on a consistent basis to sharpen one's soul.

When we do this on the mat we do it in our world. Our soul sharpened, we have more endurance in our labors, concentration in our passions, and a stronger will during physical training. Jiu Jitsu gives us the daily medium with which to combat internal weakness, giving us an honest opportunity to confront vice in an approachable and conquerable arena.

This begins but does not end on the mat. The sincerity with which we approach our training becomes the sincerity with which we live.

Nutrition is a prime example. We seek to optimize our training, and so we must be a steward of the body with which we train. We seek maximal health with sincerity. Leafy greens become opportunity, not obligation.

It is our love for Jiu Jitsu which guides our steady hand. When we eat to get the most out of our training, we eat to get the most out of life. We have more energy and less internal resistance for our passions and loved ones. Everything improves. We have more to offer and less preventing us from doing so.

There have been many times in my life when I lacked the motivation to train. My body was run down and my skill development stunted, Jiu Jitsu lost its momentary appeal. But

I always continued to show up to training, especially when I did not want to be there.

Jiu Jitsu has always come secondary to my soul. Apathy toward training could never surpass my passion to grow so I have more to give.

My pursuits always mirror my training. The sincerity with which I approach my training is generally a good indicator of how well I am succeeding in the rest of my life.

Jiu Jitsu requires a discipline and attention that transfer to every other endeavor. When we consciously pursue our development in this art, we are strengthening the muscles that we will need for the rest of our daily activities.

The closer we are able to play Jiu Jitsu with maximum efficiency, the more we are able to learn the optimization which our highest selves require. We learn to go with the stream, in the way which only we are fashioned to do.

When we develop ourselves, the outside world becomes less threatening. As our strength and confidence grow, we find the courage and discipline to be kind to others, receiving them from a place of virtue.

As we grow, so do our relationships. We develop the sincerity that others so love, a true appreciation and reciprocity of time and affection. Now that we have become someone of value, and have much to offer our fellow man, we seek to do so. We give ourselves to one another, sharing in each other's victories and defeats with genuine enthusiasm.

Without weakness, we are able to cultivate true relationships which require an integrity and vulnerability that is only found through strength. Such strength is developed from repeated opportunities to practice resolve, with each inspired action bringing us closer to whom we aspire to be.

SUMMARY OF RESOLVE AND WEAKNESS

We will never max out character development. Our potential is too great, our time too short. But we can ensure we make the most of our time, always striving to meet resistance with will and effort in the direction of the life we aspire to have.

There is rarely observable punishment for weakness in adult life. The real cost comes at the loss of life we will fail to live, the potential we squander.

Jiu Jitsu strengthens our resolve, providing us with an immune system against all which does not serve us on the way toward our highest selves. A highest self which shows its value by its ability to effect change in ourselves and the world around us, the virtue of our next coupling, efficacy.

EFFICACY AND IGNORANCE

The increase of humility and the decrease of pride gets you in the game. Improving one's resolve and removing weakness keeps you playing. But how well we play, in both Jiu Jitsu and life, is determined by our efficacy, one's ability to produce an intended result. The efficiency and effectiveness with which we make manifest our desires are the deciding factors in the creation of the life we envision.

This third and final pairing is the bridge from theory to practice. We have become someone of value, but now we must cultivate that virtue to bring this value into the material world, in the way we practice Jiu Jitsu, in the way we live our lives.

Will we achieve our aim with purposeful intent or will we languish in ignorance? The information we acquire, and our proper use of this information embodied through massive and decisive action, will lead to our highest selves. But if we operate from a place of contented ignorance, whether on the mat or in the world, we will never glimpse our potential.

> *"If you think education is expensive—try ignorance."*
> *- Derek Bok,*
> *President of Harvard University*

EFFICACY

Efficacy is the ability to achieve an intended result. This subsumes two distinct criteria, efficiency and effectiveness. Efficiency ensures we become the most with what we are given. Effectiveness ensures that that most achieves its greatest impact on our world.

With finite time to acquire skill, we seek optimization through the most efficient path, for we have no time to waste. With this efficiency, we develop great abilities, and it is our effectiveness which governs our ability to make those gifts manifest in the world.

Our efficiency and effectiveness combine to create our world. Our communication with our loved ones, our finances, our health-- in short, every aspect of our experience which we call "life"-- is governed by our ability to alter our daily experience according to a preconceived ideal.

This is the measure of all skill, the ability to create what is intended. We hone this skill in grappling. Every moment of training enables us to actualize our will in the face of resistance, as we constantly gain experience by bending experience, or the body of our partner, to our will.

My time on the mats is when I act most efficiently and effectively in the world. The daily reps of moving with such precision and intent give me invaluable experience of optimizing my will, an ability which shapes the rest of my world.

I never realized how inefficient I was until I began my study of this art. Inefficient in everything: my communication, my exercise, my organization, and my studies. There are countless ways to perform Jiu Jitsu, with varying games and styles based off one's abilities, but each of those styles of gameplay is best expressed with maximum efficiency.

We learn to be efficient because effective Jiu Jitsu requires it. Skilled training partners will not allow anything else.

Life rarely offers such immediate feedback for our efforts. In Jiu Jitsu, we collect data immediately, our fatigue serving as our most accurate metric. The resistance we meet in every movement reveals the purity of our position, timing, and movement. We can constantly feel the value of our efforts with a tangible proof of their validity.

This efficiency allows for maximum effectiveness. The environment demands it. We do not get this in any other area of life, which explains why we are often so ineffective at creating change.

Consider one's academic curriculum. In adult life, very few (if any) people care what you are reading, how often you read, and with what degree of sincerity. No one is there to stop you from repeatedly checking your smart phone or turning on the TV when study becomes difficult.

This reveals one of the great truths of the human experience:

We never see our greatest failures because they exist as missed opportunities.

We cannot experience non-experience; without becoming what we could have been, we possess no measuring stick with which to gauge how far we have fallen from our potential. We exist as we are, never realizing what we could be.

"Man, proud man, drest in a little brief authority--
Most ignorant of what he's most assured,
His glassy essence--like an angry ape,
Plays such fantastic tricks before high heaven
As make the angels weep."
-William Shakespeare

Most ignorant of what he's most assured. This truth reveals the dire need for our study of grappling. We cannot hide in ignorance; the truth reveals itself in every roll.

The Jiu Jitsu academy is organized to systematically remove this ignorance. We have instructors whose sole focus is to teach us the intricacies of the art, ensuring we move farther along the continuum of efficiency. We are actively managed by those more knowledgeable than ourselves-- our parents of grappling, but we are no longer self-righteous teenagers.

Our instructors give us the tools to train efficiently but our real world application of these concepts is contingent upon the resistance our partners offer.

When training with a partner, no matter the position, we act against resistance. The effectiveness of our actions results from the efficiency with which we perform them. If I am trying to pass the guard, and I meet great resistance, the data collected shows me that an alternative path is a more appropriate route. At a certain point in every position, we must try something different rather than try the same technique with more physicality.

And sometimes the movement toward efficiency is subtle: a little off balance, a slight adjustment of grip, faking left before going right. Each position presents a different opportunity to solve a different puzzle in the most productive way.

This is the proper mindset with which to view our training partners. While on the mat, they are not people; they are puzzles. Each is like a different level of a video game, offering different forms of resistance, possessing various strengths and weaknesses unlike any other, each yielding a different form of growth.

Even those people you don't like training with present a worthy puzzle. The guys who run and run, perpetually failing to disengage, offer a wonderful opportunity to perform our Jiu Jitsu against one who refuses to engage in Jiu Jitsu. Though these guys are not the most enjoyable to train with, they are a problem whose solution proves invaluable in our ability to bend experience to our will.

Jiu Jitsu ingrains in our being that efficiency is beauty; inefficiency is ugliness. When I move in a sub-optimal way, relying on some physical attribute rather than proper technique, I feel dirty, as though I just cheated on Jiu Jitsu.

When we move inefficiently, we tarnish the beauty. When we move optimally, with the current of the stream, with perfect timing and expression, Providence moves. We no longer resist circumstance and readily accept whatever experience we are having.

When we do this in grappling, we learn to do it in life. Maybe not consciously at first, and it may take years to notice the benefits, but they'll be there. Because, once we develop the sincerity that causes inefficient movements to feel dirty in Jiu Jitsu, that feeling will slowly work its way into our everyday lives.

> *"The cost of a thing is the amount of what I will call life required to be exchanged for it, either immediately or in the long run."*
> -Henry David Thoreau

Inefficiency costs us a portion of our finite life.

Neglecting meal prep for the week results in unnecessary hours spent in preparing meals which could have been put toward our passions. The simple inefficiencies of daily searching for our car keys, over a lifetime, come at sizeable cost. Inattention to communication with our loved ones robs us of the beauty of our relationships.

Again, we possess no measuring stick with which to gauge the efficiency of our actions, because we measure them against an unseen ideal, our highest selves we fail to achieve.

Jiu Jitsu reveals optimal action. There is a crispness to the movement, a divinity behind it. Performing an action in the best way at the most opportune time, we learn to interact with experience in the most productive and effortless way, a flowing with what the eastern mystics call the "Tao."

This knowledge gives us the ability to recognize when we act with such precision in our daily lives, but more often, however, this knowledge reveals our inefficiency in the world, a priceless gift which only perspective offers.

We do not always have to know what better is to realize that we can do better. Sometimes knowing that our current mode of action is lacking is enough to fuel us onward to new discoveries of our potential.

> *"All arts, big and small, are the elimination of waste motion in favor of the concise declaration. The artist learns what to leave out."*
> *-Ray Bradbury*

Black belt, if nothing else, is a movement toward efficiency. When we describe someone as a "black belt" in anything, we acknowledge their efficiency in achieving maximal effectiveness. Anyone who is great at anything is great because of his ability to perform an action against with the least possible resistance, both internal and external.

Our efficiency in grappling reveals our inefficiency everywhere else. And it also reveals our standards for such effectiveness. Imagine if we paid the sincere attention to our finances and relationships as we do guard passing.

Any wasted movement on the mat feels ugly. I chastise myself and demand constant improvement. But I accept those same weaknesses which manifest in my adult life, paying them no mind. It took becoming a black belt in Jiu Jitsu to realize that I am a white belt in everything else.

Jiu Jitsu trains our ability to optimize. When we learn to play Jiu Jitsu in this way, we become capable of living this way in the world. Nothing exists in a vacuum. Our focus muscles are present in every labor. When efficiency and effectiveness become the foundation of our world, we become capable of changing that world.

IGNORANCE

Life will continue to try to teach us the same lesson, with increasing pain, until we heed the message. Many of us find ourselves making the same mistakes throughout our lifetime, our failures sharing similar themes.

Tony Robbins says that success leaves clues; well, so does failure. There is an interwoven thread that traces through all the mistakes in my life, and it almost always stems from an impatience and inability to view the task at hand objectively. Before Jiu Jitsu, I would chalk up these repeated failures to circumstance. *Things don't always go as hoped*. But a clearer lens shows my shortcomings are caused by failures of thinking, not chance.

There are countless variables in Jiu Jitsu but all positions and techniques are expressions of a handful of fundamental concepts. Jiu Jitsu has shown me that my failures on the mat, getting my guard passed or being submitted, result from a chain of events and countless missed opportunities to alter circumstance.

We should make mistakes, but we should learn from them, stand on the foundation of the new understanding they create, and make better mistakes in the future.

*"Saint Augustine! well hast thou said,
That of our vices we can frame
A ladder, if we will but tread
Beneath our feet each deed of shame!"
-The Ladder of St. Augustine, Henry Wadsword Longfellow*

There is no valid excuse for making the same mistake or getting caught with the same technique. If we have the underlying knowledge base with which to clearly identify the problem, and we fail to adjust, we are the problem. Our failure is simply a lack of attention and likely a microcosm of our relationship to our world.

We bring these same subjective, suboptimal tendencies into every profession, relationship, or role we embody. Our activities are ways in which we express ourselves, revealing our depths; our unencumbered shortcomings leaving a trail of missteps in their wake.

Jiu Jitsu has shown me that these continued misfortunes are due to my lack of attention and purposefully directed thought, not circumstance.

If I get guillotined while trying to pass the guard, there is a succession of steps which led to that event. I left my neck out while passing. I allowed my partner's back to get off the mat. I wasn't chest to chest.

I am having an experience, but not a relationship to the experience. Wisdom is this relationship, ignorance is to remain uninitiated.

And this is how we so often live the rest of our lives. We make the same mistakes in our relationships and our professions. Rather than dissect a problem, we offer it up to fate. *That's just the way things are.* But they exist in this way solely because we don't attend to a solution.

Jiu Jitsu has taught me causality in a way western philosophy never could. I see that a succession of steps must occur to reach a particular end.

Jiu Jitsu no longer allows me to neglect this truth in the rest of my experience. Excuses carry no more internal validation.

All human activities consist of similar fundamentals and concepts. We only come to know this when we have ventured deeply down one road, and then walk down another, and realize that their differing landscapes hide the fact that all roads toward mastery parallel one another, with more commonalities than differences.

The depths we have explored in Jiu Jitsu help us see that we remain in the shallows in most other endeavors. We can only appreciate the mastery of another in proportion to the degree we have mastered something ourselves.

This awareness leaves no place for the pleading of ignorance. We realize, in the words of Ernest Henley, that we are the masters of our fate.

> *This is what Jiu Jitsu really teaches: the personal accountability to demand resolution in the face of unfavorable conditions.*

Every undesirable experience during a roll results from a previously unaddressed mistake. The same holds true in the rest of our lives, but without someone seeking to take immediate advantage of our folly, we are not forced to correct our course.

The great chasm which exists between who we are and who we could someday become is widened by our subtle daily habits each day. They are so seemingly insignificant that we often don't even acknowledge their presence. Only years later do we learn the cumulative effect of our inattention.

Though my knowledge is limited, I possess a foundation solid enough from which to interpret my training. When I make a mistake, I can quickly trace the preceding events which led to that folly. I am then able to learn and grow from the experience. And if I can't make sense of it, I don't have to travel far to find someone who can.

All our problems consist of several smaller problems. These digestible pieces of the whole allow us to break down our experience, learn the fundamentals which have been expressed, and apply this new understanding in other areas of our lives.

When I fail to do this, I am making a choice. I am choosing to neglect useful information which will improve my experience. By failing to attend to the details, I miss out on the opportunity for growth which they present.

Jiu Jitsu trains us to solve problems in the most efficient and effective way. The more we operate from this lens on the mat, the more likely we are to approach the rest of our lives in such a reasonable way.

Whenever we operate from a place of ignorance, we impede our highest selves. This ignorance is the source of much of the pain we cause one another.

I have always viewed people's maltreatment of myself in a simple way. If someone harms me out of ignorance, I cannot fault their action. They did not intend to hurt me, and with life's many complexities and limitless variables to attend to, I understand that I may be a casualty of their efforts.

"People aren't against you; they are for themselves."

Now, if they act out of malice, with the purposeful intent of doing me harm, this is also out of ignorance. Perhaps even more so. Our language reveals our world, as the word "sin" translated in Latin is "to miss the mark."

One cannot cause more pain to another than they themselves already feel. If someone hurts me out of ignorance, that's okay. In the end, everyone is doing the best of which they are capable in that moment. As I daily struggle to live in the most virtuous way, and repeatedly fall short, it is not hard to empathize when another does the same. Nothing, it is revealed, is personal.

REVIEW OF THE THREE PAIRS

It is these three pairings which constitute the bulk of our humanity.

Thus far, these virtues have been focused on ourselves. Our focus has been to craft our own character, to achieve a greater self than we once were. A self free of our natural imperfections, now capable of effecting great change in the world.

Ultimately, our efforts are only worthwhile to the degree they benefit others. As we advance along these three continuums, we find that one more virtue is needed to warrant such focus on self.

Generosity is the bridge with which we take our newly cultivated self and give it away. Our highest self can only be found among the collective. Our contribution to the group defines the worth of our private actions.

GENEROSITY

The cultivation of the previous virtues gives us something to offer others, but it is generosity which allows us to give it away.

Jiu Jitsu has taught me a generosity that I had never before embodied. I am inherently self-centered. It has taken a great deal of study and the benefit of wonderful parents to bring me to a place where it feels natural to think about others as I do myself. I had to read many books just to arrive where so many of my dear friends began.

Jiu Jitsu shatters these self-centered tendencies. When we first begin our practice in an organized setting, we are partnered with senior-most students, who act as our ferrymen, guiding us to that distance shore of understanding of this craft. For many of us, this is the only time throughout the day that someone devotes his time and energy to serve us.

We rarely communicate this experience but we all feel it. The kindness of our mentor breaks down our inner walls which prevent us from receiving, and giving, that generosity.

I tend to allocate my time very selectively, spending as much time as possible in purposefully chosen acts. This is a source of my greatest strength and weakness. This singularity of attention gives me the ability to develop myself so I have more to offer others, but is often the very mechanism with which I ignore those to whom I wish to be of service.

But this is never the case with Jiu Jitsu. I step on to a mat, and I am excited to answer other's questions and spend my time in helping them better understand this art. I freely trade the next round of live training to review the previous role with my partner. This was the example set by those before me, a practice I now happily continue. This selflessness on the mat facilitates the same action in daily life.

One of my favorite books is *Joshua*, a fictional tale about Jesus returning today, describing how he would treat others and how he would be treated. There is one section which highlights my greatest failure. It reads:

> *"As he passed, he called out to Joshua. Joshua turned and waved. When Herm started to talk to him, Joshua dropped his hoe and walked over to the fence. He was always ready to stop what he was doing and spend a few minutes socializing. It was almost as if that was his real business."*

I daily fail to act with such love. When I am reading and writing, I shut out the outside world, even responding aversely to a loved one who interjects on my study. Winning achievements but neglecting loved ones, it will be those moments I most regret on my death bed.

But Jiu Jitsu is helping me work through this natural inclination toward self-centeredness. When I spend some time after training to help a junior student learn a concept, I am much more likely to put down the book that night when my roommate walks into the room. Jiu Jitsu allows me to get reps in the practice of the virtue I need more than any other and will be the bridge that spreads generosity through the rest of my life.

There is no better use of one's time than to serve our fellow man. This is the "love your neighbor as yourself" which is so easy to understand but so hard to practice.

It's not easy and goes against our natural programming. However, given enough time, these seized opportunities shift our focus from ourselves toward others. It is only then that true relationships can be forged.

I have found no better vehicle with which to practice this outer-directedness than Jiu Jitsu.

CHAPTER 3

Why We Grow

FRIENDSHIP

Friendship has always been a pillar of happiness. There is simply no more reliable or time-tested mood-enhancer than time spent with those you love.

> *"To the Ancients, Friendship seemed the happiest and most fully human of all loves; the crown of life and the school of virtue. The modern world, in comparison, ignores it."*
> - C.S. Lewis

We rarely purposefully attend to our relationships like we do our investment portfolio or our fitness plan. Our culture commonly prescribes more materialistic modes of achieving happiness, subtly devaluing our perception of friendship. Without proper value placed on strengthening these ties, they often wither out of neglect.

Jiu Jitsu creates friendships of a sincerity that our daily lives rarely match. Shared suffering toward a common goal profoundly influences our connection with another human being. When we recognize how much we love Jiu Jitsu, and we see that love shared by our teammates, this bonds us at our depths that transcend the superficial differences of history, occupation, and age.

> *"Friendship... is born at the moment when one man says to another, 'What! You too? I thought that no one but myself...'"*
> -C.S. Lewis

It is that unique interest which binds us. The majority of the people we encounter on a daily basis have no interest in Jiu Jitsu; half of them think it's Karate. The deep passion we share for Jiu Jitsu connects us.

And it is this shared love which allows us to suffer over a prolonged period of time. This suffering forges our bonds to one another. I am closest to those teammates with whom I train the most, the ones who share a similar standard for themselves and pursue their potential to whatever degree they are capable. Our paths parallel one another's.

Our shared sacrifice helps us find community in struggle. When fellowship is forged in mutual suffering toward a freely chosen aim, an atmosphere of the collective accelerates relationships and strengthens their bond.

Friendship is an odd mix of dependency and appreciation.

I find that my friendships in this art often stem from an initial self-centeredness. We are only as good as our training partners, our skill and progress in Jiu Jitsu are directly linked to the efforts of our peer group. Selfishly, we must help our partners grow.

The only way to traverse the path is to walk it together. Sometimes we are pushed and sometimes we are pulling, but we go together.

This dependency forms a sense of team unlike anything we experience in team sports.

Whether through selfishness or altruism, we must sincerely wish that our teammates achieve excellence. Our growth demands it.

This dependence becomes appreciation. We share the same aches and pains. We each sacrifice much time and attention for this art. Only those on the same path know what it is to walk.

Direct experience can never be communicated. Most of my relationships are not centered around Jiu Jitsu. Many know nothing about the art I love so dearly. And this holds true for just about all of us. Most with whom we interact on a daily basis do not share our passion, and therefore communicate a different set of values through a different language than we do.

We meet on the periphery of our passions when we come up for air in the real world, but we rarely share our richest depths with those so close to us. This is the significance of our relationships with our teammates. We can connect over something so meaningful which we so often fail to share with others.

My core group of training partners share a connectedness I haven't found outside of Jiu Jitsu. When you go so far down the same path, your paths tend to merge. In the ways that matter, you become one.

> *"Friendship must be about something... Those who have nothing can share nothing; those who are going nowhere have no fellow travelers."*
> *- C.S. Lewis*

I have found that through our shared love of Jiu Jitsu, my closest friends and I have come to love one another. Our relationships began centered around Jiu Jitsu; now Jiu Jitsu serves as the unseen foundation upon which our relationships continue to build. We will spend days together and never once mention grappling. Jiu Jitsu lies so squarely at the center of our friendship that we often forget it's there.

These friendships come together to form a communal love within the group. With many working together toward the same end, we find a union with a group external to ourselves, creating a community in which we pursue self-actualization together.

Friendship exists between individuals, but when those many pairings of like minds come together in a larger group, those individual friendships forge something far greater, fellowship.

FELLOWSHIP

Man needs fellowship. We are pack animals who pretend to be solitary creatures.

Fellowship once came in our tribe, then in small communities, and the anchor through most of the western world, the church. The secular world, however, seems to offer very few means of fellowship which positively serve the growth of the individual.

Spectator sports and local bars bring people together, but often at the price, whether direct or through opportunity cost, of the individual. We've lost this sense of community and replaced it with depression and loneliness. It is connection with others which staves off such suffering.

We find our truest self among a collective which helps procure that uniqueness from our depths. We come to appreciate each other's unique abilities, becoming curators of each other's talents, offering an external aid in self-actualization.

Jiu Jitsu gives us this community. In a judgment-free environment, we lose the need to defend ourselves, allowing for transcendence of that self.

Where else can so many people from different walks of life come together to purposefully fail through great physical and mental exertion? We praise a teammate for whooping us. We love them for it. Nowhere else in the secular world do we find so many people striving together toward the highest version of themselves.

And that's the magic sauce which sustains our group. We each choose to be there. We carve out time, energy, attention, and money for Jiu Jitsu. We pay, with all of life's currencies, to be there. But it really isn't for Jiu Jitsu, is it?

We make this sacrifice for our soul, knowing that our highest self is found in a community of others. We are fully dependent upon one another for all of Maslow's pyramid. Our success in life is determined by the success of our peer group.

Jiu Jitsu gives us a community in which to find ourselves and to offer that self to others.

Our teammates are our family, sharing in our passion as well as our pain. We understand each other's depths, fulfilling the psychological need of belonging to a tribe. We need the influence of others to become what only we can be.

When we look closely, we see that we need the influence of every single member of the tribe. Everyone serves a purpose. Everyone presents a gift. Years ago, my dear friend Pete McHugh mentioned in passing what has guided much of my philosophy.

"Everyone plays a role in the academy."

Every member of the tribe is of importance. There are obvious roles, like the senior instructors and experienced students setting the culture of the school, or the program direct keeping a roof over our heads, but we each play a part. The jerk no one wants to train with is a binding agent within the group-- when the community's values are threatened, the tribe's bonds deepen. The brand new white belt gives us an opportunity to aid and instruct, practicing patience while we assist another. And even the resident goofball adds the much-needed comic relief from daily struggle.

Everyone serves a purpose within the academy. Every single teammate, whether you consider him a friend or not, plays a serious role in creating the community in which you pursue your highest self. We owe our continued growth, and subsequent gratitude, to each of them.

When we come to understand this in the Jiu Jitsu community, we have a sense of unifying purpose. We play an important function in something greater than ourselves. We are better equipped to handle adversity, as we are guided by a cause external to ourselves.

Awareness of this truth in the academy leads to our final shift in perspective: seeing this truth in our world.

THE HUMAN ORGANISM

All the work on ourselves, and the generosity with which we share that new self with the world, all lead to this final understanding: the multitudes of men and women which comprise our species all constitute the completeness of the one humanity.

Humanity in a single organism, of which we are but a cell. We are connected in ways we cannot see. All that we possess is a result of the efforts of everyone who has come before us. Our influence extends far beyond those with whom we interact, leaving ripples which travel indefinitely into the future.

While we are here, with whatever time we have, we must contribute to this organism of which we are but a small part.

> *"How can I contribute?" is a noble question. "How can I best contribute?" is nobler still.*

Our striving toward virtue and the removal of vice is only worthwhile to the degree that we benefit others. Whatever we are fashioned to be, we must be that. Becoming a second-rate version of someone else serves no one, the world already has that gift in the form of the first-rate man of whom we fall short.

Our task is to fulfill the role which only we can play. There is no task too small, as each is of equal value in the context of the whole.

In the human body, the heart is no more or less important than the lungs. Each organ works in unison to comprise the whole of the organism. The most powerful heart in the world, without lungs to oxygenate the blood, is worthless. The value of the organ is found in relation to, and conjunction with, all the others.

Our lives are no different. We are each fashioned to play a specific role within the fabric of humanity. We have the freedom to neglect this responsibility. The world will march on just fine without our efforts, but for each of us who does not fulfill our potential, the world will be a little less beautiful than it could have been.

Whatever you are fashioned to be, whether an engineer, a dancer, a mom, or a florist, you can create beauty and value through this endeavor using the gifts you have been given. It is the best thing you can do for yourself and the best thing you can do for the whole.

The more efficiently each of the cells of humanity work, and toward the aim that each of us is most inclined to create value, the greater this world will be. And when we know our most optimal function within society, we are afforded an amazing gift. We are given the opportunity to serve in the unique fashion for which we were created.

> *"Service is love made visible."*
> *- Stephen Colbert*

The world is in a tumultuous time. The human organism is fractured, its many cells angry, disenfranchised, and disconnected from the whole. It is in these times of difficulty that we must seek our own goodness.

We are the white blood cells of humanity, fighting off disease so the organism can prosper. The disease we battle is of the mind. Bad ideas are taking root in the world. We are becoming increasingly disconnected from one another, with countless distractions with which to throw away our time. It appears much of modern culture-- the sugar, the sitting, the television, the apps on our phones-- whether intentional or not, rob us of our greatest individuality and highest expression of our potential.

> *It has never been so easy to do the wrong things.*

We have a dire responsibility to our fellow man. Those of us who constantly seek to exceed ourselves improve the human organism. If one cell in the body improves, the body in its totality improves. As you grow so does the humanity with contains you. When we are aware of this, we understand that we have a personal responsibility to the rest of humanity to become the highest possible version of ourselves.

Not many will notice if you don't. Few will care. Maybe you don't care. But if you fall short of your potential, the world is objectively worse for your having done so.

There is no such thing as maintenance. If we do not move closer toward our best, we are actively moving in the other direction. Whenever we choose the lower, all-too-accessible path of comfort, we do so at a cost to everyone whom we hold so dear.

This is a hard way to live, bearing the weight of your daily decisions within the context of the entire fabric of humanity. We needn't keep this truth in the forefront of our minds all day. But remembering this when making the big decisions will give us a constant metric with which to determine the value of our actions. And then, without our even realizing it, we start to see the far-reaching effects of those subtle, little choices throughout the day, which go unnoticed, but shape our destiny.

We bring our best gifts into the world so that others may benefit.

The ancient hero of myth always returns from his journey with a boon to bestow upon the community. The community's sacrifice in his absence is made worthwhile by the treasure he returns with. The time we spend working on ourselves is only valuable to the degree with which it improves the lives of others.

Our purpose exceeds ourselves.

Jiu Jitsu allows us to fulfill this purpose, the vehicle with which we carve our soul, by becoming the highest version of ourselves. It is that self, forged on the mats with those we love, who is made ready for service.

The fate of the world depends on the quality of people that we become. I will teach this beautiful art until my body crumbles. I just cannot envision any of us receiving the benefits of Jiu Jitsu from any other source. Our greatest humanity can only be found in the environment Jiu Jitsu provides.

Jiu Jitsu allows me to be of service to others. Nothing has ever brought me more joy. Your service will be contingent upon you, not your medium. The effectiveness with which you play your role is limited by the capacity of your soul. Jiu Jitsu trains these depths, crafting the fiber of our being, creating a strength that is only derived from an environment as worthwhile, dense, and arduous as Jiu Jitsu.

It doesn't matter what you do. What matters is that you do it, with as much strength and kindness as you are capable. Jiu Jitsu builds us up so we have more to give. The longer we train, the more hours we have spent carving our soul, and the more we will have to share with the rest of the world.

No man is an island. In ways we cannot understand, we are each connected in the fabric of the one humanity. We are all expressions of that single body that spans the continents and the generations.

We are part of a much larger dance. We are just starting to hear the music. It's a gift to have the floor, no matter how brief. While we have it, it is our responsibility to dance as only we can, performing the best we are capable of, in the way in which we are fashioned to do so.

We are too limited in our perspective to grasp the significance of our training. Our time spent on the mat is time spent molding our humanity. We bring the same self into every interaction-- to the grocery store, to the in-laws, to your wife or husband at dinner and to your friends on the weekends. The quality of every experience is contingent upon he who does the experiencing. Our lives are only as beautiful as we are.

I have never met a man, woman, or child who did not benefit from their time in this art. Jiu Jitsu brings each one of us closer to our potential. This understanding deepens our relationship to our craft, the foundation of the attention and respect we bring to our practice. But we do so not to master Jiu Jitsu. We do this to master ourselves.

CONCLUSION

I believe the best philosophies are the simplest. This is mine:

> *We have a personal responsibility, as members of the collective, to grow and become the highest version of ourselves, and to use that self in the service of others.*

This modus operandi, when sincerely and purposefully pursued, achieves all that is worthwhile in its fulfillment. We are most happy, and most spirited, when we are learning and growing. In seeking mastery of a skill, we come to better know ourselves, cultivating a mastery of our own character. Through the purposeful pursuit of skill-acquisition, we magnify and multiply our virtues, hacking away at the roots of our vices, as we move close toward our most actualized self. In the end, however, all the time spent in study is only worthwhile to the degree that other's benefit from our efforts.

We are here to live for each other. The saints and sages of the past agree that freedom from suffering is found when we focus on the well-being of others. While looking outward, we free ourselves from our natural inclination toward self-centeredness, the cause of our suffering.

Once we have acquired value, through effort and ceaseless struggle, we give that value to our beloved through whatever means we are fashioned to do so. The successful man is he, who, having developed great skill in his chosen craft, performs that skill, with love, gratitude, and great deft, in the service of his fellow man.

This must be our aspiration. We have a responsibility to each other to seek our highest selves. Humanity improves in proportion to the growth of the humans which comprise it.

I'll become a better me for you, if you become a better you for me.

Behavior modification is difficult. We often fail to facilitate the changes we seek. The right choices meet the least resistance when we focus on others. We are inextricably linked. We must be a steward of our greatest gifts so that we can be a gift to our fellow man.

This is the immeasurable value that Jiu Jitsu provides. Our time in this art is more worthwhile than we can possibly fathom. The people we've met, the experiences we've had, and who we have become along the way, are the fruits of our labor.

Jiu Jitsu is a gift from Grace. Such blessings come with great responsibility. We must use this art to doggedly strive toward our highest selves, becoming beacons of good in the world.

Become the best version of yourself, then give that self away. Jiu Jitsu is the vehicle, and above all else, we drive for each other.

.

NOTES

NOTES

NOTES

NOTES

NOTES

NOTES

NOTES

NOTES

Made in the USA
Lexington, KY
29 November 2017